Landslides and Avalanches

By Jim and Ronda Redmond

A Harcourt Company

Austin · New York
www.steck-vaughn.com

Published by Raintree Steck-Vaughn Publishers, an imprint of Steck-Vaughn Company.

Library of Congress Cataloging-in-Publication Data (need from RSVP)
    Landslides and avalanches/by Jim Redmond, Ronda Redmond.
        p.cm.—(Nature on the rampage)
    Includes bibliographical references and index.
    ISBN 0-7398-4704-X
    1. Landslides—Juvenile literature. 2. Avalanches—Juvenile literature.
[1. Landslides. 2. Avalanches.] I. Redmond, Ronda. II. Title. III. Series.

200101

Printed and bound in the United States of America
1 2 3 4 5 6 7 8 9 10 WZ 05 04 03 02 01

Produced by Compass Books

Photo Acknowledgments
Corbis/Chris Rainier, 8; AFP, 26
NOAA, title page, 4, 7, 12, 20, 24
Root Resources/Doug Sherman, 17, 29
Unicorn Stock Photos/A Ramey, 23
Visuals Unlimited/Peter Dunwidde, cover

Content Consultants
Lynn Highland
United States Geological Society
National Landslide Information Center

Maria Kent Rowell
Science Consultant
Sebastopol, California

David Larwa
National Science Education Consultant;
Educational Training Services
Brighton, Michigan

This book supports the National Science Standards.

▼ CONTENTS

Some landslides sweep cars off roads. They can also damage huge parts of roads.

WHEN EARTH SLIDES

Wherever there are hills or mountains, mass wasting can happen. Mass wasting is the natural transfer of rock or soil downslope. Rocks, dirt, or mud speed down a **slope** during a **landslide**. Snow and ice race downslope during an avalanche. Every state in the United States has had a landslide or avalanche. However, they are most common in Alaska, Hawaii, and around mountains.

We do not know the exact number of landslides and avalanches that happen each year. Many times, they occur far away from people. Scientists think that almost 500,000 landslides and one million avalanches sweep down mountains every year.

Landslides

Many landslides form during the rainy season or when snow melts in spring. Earth falls whenever soil and rock is no longer able to hold together on a hillside or mountainside. Then, gravity makes the earth slide. Gravity is a force that pulls things toward the center of our planet and keeps them from floating away into space. There are many different ways earth can move down slopes, including debris flows, rockslides and falls, flows, **slumps**, and **creeps**.

Debris flows, or lahars, are among the fastest and most powerful kind of landslide. Debris flows are often caused when a volcano erupts. They are made of water and volcanic debris, such as mud, ash, and rock. They often come without any warning, so people have little time to move to safety.

A rockslide is a landslide made up of falling rocks. Mud and wet clay form liquid-like flows.

Slumps and creeps are slower and take less land with them. A slump happens when a

▲ **This hillside has been damaged by a creep.**

section of a hillside moves down a short distance. It stops where the soil and rock pile. A creep happens over a large area of land.

Slumps and creeps can move as slowly as 0.5 inch (1.3 cm) each year. Over time, slumps and creeps can damage buildings, roads, fences, and railroad tracks.

▲ This avalanche is sweeping down a mountain in the Swiss Alps.

Avalanches

Avalanches happen after winter snowstorms and in the spring. They generally happen in January, February, and March.

Layers of snow can create different kinds of avalanches. Every time snow falls, it creates a new layer. A single mountainside

Rescuers use dogs to find people who have been buried by avalanches. Dogs can find scents even if they are covered by many feet of snow. A Saint Bernard named Barry found 40 people who were buried by avalanches.

can have many layers of snow. All the layers together are called a snowpack.

Two kinds of avalanches are sluff avalanches and slab avalanches. Sluff avalanches are made up of the top layer of loose snow. These avalanches happen most often after a snowstorm when the new layer of light snow slides down a mountain. They usually form a triangle-shape as they spread.

Slab avalanches are the most powerful and deadly of avalanches. All the layers of a snowpack can fall at once during a slab avalanche. Large slab avalanches can carry up to one million tons of snow and ice down a mountain. Within seconds, the avalanche races along at speeds of up to 100 miles (161 km) per hour. Strong, dangerous winds build up ahead of the fall.

Path of an Avalanche

The way an avalanche moves down a mountain or hill is called its path. Each avalanche has its own path. Some are wide, while others are narrow. Some run straight, while others zigzag down the mountain.

All avalanche paths are made up of three parts. These are the starting zone, the track, and the runout zone. The avalanche begins at the starting zone. This place is usually high on a mountain or hill where a great deal of snow falls. As the snow piles higher, it gets heavier and heavier until it slides.

The track is the path an avalanche takes downhill. Avalanches move fast down the **steep,** or very tall, track. They often tear down all trees and plants there.

The runout zone is the end of the avalanche path. The avalanche slows down and stops in the runout zone, leaving all of its ice, snow, and rocks there.

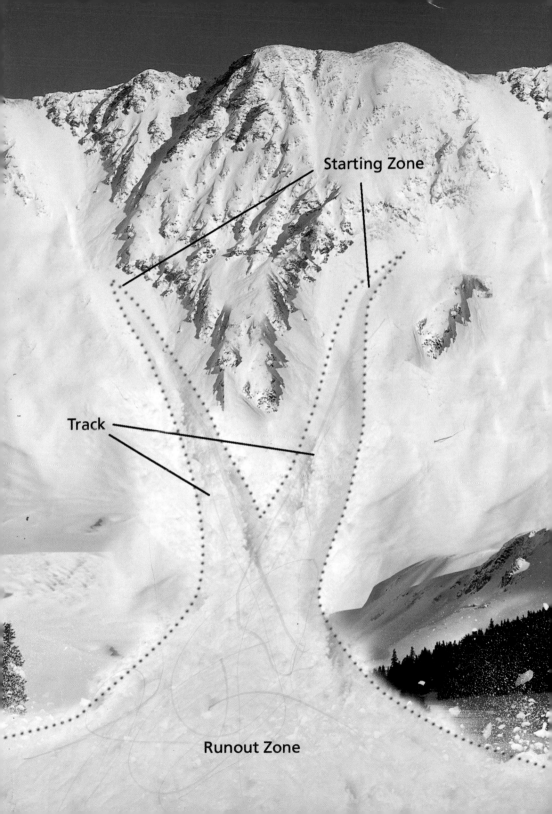

Starting Zone

Track

Runout Zone

A mudslide has buried part of this house in mud.

What Landslides and Avalanches Do

Landslides and avalanches tear trees out by the roots, crush houses, and move cars and huge rocks. When these slides stop, they may bury whole towns under tons of dirt, mud, or snow. Many people and animals are also swept away or buried. It is hard for rescuers to reach people trapped by these slides. The slides often block roads. They may cause whole sections of road to slide downhill.

People caught in avalanches face dangers. They can crash into trees and rocks as they fall downhill. If they live through the fall, they can be buried and suffocate. Suffocate means to run out of air to breathe.

People who are rescued can still die from **hypothermia**. Hypothermia occurs when the body's temperature falls too far below normal. If they do not get help fast enough, they will freeze to death. Only one out of ten people who are caught in an avalanche live.

Landslides can flow into rivers. When this happens, the landslide blocks the river and stops water from flowing past it. The water might build up behind the landslide until it breaks free and floods the areas around it.

As slides fall, they leave **scars**, or bare paths. The snow and dirt in these places are likely to fall again.

Snow falls and covers a slope in layers.

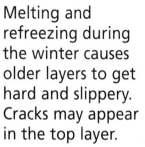

Melting and refreezing during the winter causes older layers to get hard and slippery. Cracks may appear in the top layer.

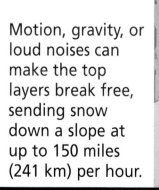

Motion, gravity, or loud noises can make the top layers break free, sending snow down a slope at up to 150 miles (241 km) per hour.

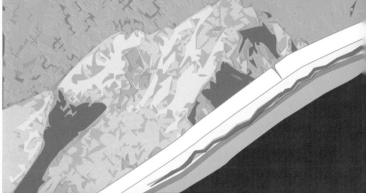

This diagram shows what can cause an avalanche.

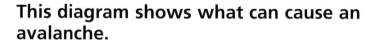

What Causes Slides?

People sometimes cause landslides when they build houses on hillsides. When they do this, they pack the dirt lower on the hill, so it will hold the weight of the house. Sometimes they also build stone or cement walls to help hold the hill in place. When all of this is not done correctly, landslides could happen.

People also cause landslides when they cut down too many trees. Without tree roots to help hold dirt in place, landslides can easily happen.

Skiers can cause avalanches by skiing on snow that is **unstable,** or loose. The snow may seem fine on top, but there could be weak snow under the top layer.

Natural Causes of Landslides

Landslides are more likely to happen on steep hills and mountains. The taller the hill or mountain, the harder it is for trees and plants to hold things in place.

Landslides are common in certain types of soils. Sometimes layers of loose gravel or clay are under the topsoil. These layers may become slippery and cause a landslide.

Earthquakes are one cause of landslides. When earthquakes happen, they break up the ground. This can cause big hunks of earth to fall down the hill. They can also loosen large pieces of rock and boulders.

Weather can also cause landslides. When a lot of rain falls in a short time, the dirt turns into mud and becomes heavy. Sometimes tree and plant roots are not enough to hold the mud in place, and a **mudslide** forms.

Rockslides often happen when the weather turns from cold to warm. In the winter, water freezes around rocks and in rock cracks. When water freezes, it **expands,**

▲ **A rockslide has buried this house.**

or grows larger. The ice in some cracks grows big enough to split the rocks. In the spring, when the water melts, chunks of rock can break off and fall down a hill.

Floods can also cause landslides. During floods, rivers become wider. A river may wash away the plants and dirt at the bottom of a hill. Without dirt and plants at the bottom, chunks of the hilltop will fall and cause a slide.

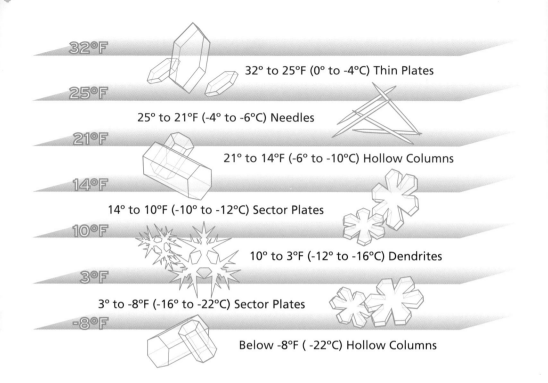

32°F

32° to 25°F (0° to -4°C) Thin Plates

25°F

25° to 21°F (-4° to -6°C) Needles

21°F

21° to 14°F (-6° to -10°C) Hollow Columns

14°F

14° to 10°F (-10° to -12°C) Sector Plates

10°F

10° to 3°F (-12° to -16°C) Dendrites

3°F

3° to -8°F (-16° to -22°C) Sector Plates

-8°F

Below -8°F (-22°C) Hollow Columns

This diagram shows ice-crystal shapes and the temperatures in which they form.

What Causes Avalanches?

To understand how an avalanche starts, you must know about different kinds of snow. All snow is made of tiny ice crystals. These crystals are different shapes depending on the kind of snow. Some ice-crystal shapes help snow stick together better. Heavy snow holds together well. Light snow does not stick to other kinds of snow well. Because of this, light snow slides easier than other snow.

Layers of light and heavy snow often cause avalanches. For example, avalanches may happen when heavy snow falls on top of light snow or light snow falls on heavy snow.

Temperature changes also cause avalanches. Warmer and cooler temperatures can make the ice crystals change shape. Some layers of snow then become unstable because they do not stick to each other. When a top layer of snow slips off a bottom layer, it creates a sluff avalanche.

Winter storms with heavy snowfalls can cause avalanches. The weight of new snow may make old snow break away from the mountainside and slide downhill.

Wind is a common cause of avalanches. The wind blows loose snow from one part of the mountain and places it on another part. Over time, the snow collects until it becomes too heavy and starts an avalanche.

A past landslide has left this scar through the forest.

SLIDES IN HISTORY

Slides have happened throughout Earth's history. We know that people told stories called legends to explain these natural events.

People who lived around mountains told stories about **gnomes**. In legends, gnomes are tiny people, about 15 inches (38 cm) tall, who live inside mountains. Gnomes made jewelry out of gold and special stones. When they were angry, they did things to upset people, such as throwing rocks down the mountains. People believed these rocks started slides.

In Greenland, stories about gnomes are a little different. They still started avalanches, but then they rode on top of the avalanches as the slides were going downhill.

California

California has a history of deadly landslides. It is one of the states that has been hit the hardest. These slides happen for many reasons.

There are many hills in California. Earthquakes and heavy rainfalls make the soil and rocks on hillsides ready to slide. Since people build houses in the hills, they may be weakened even more. Hills in California have underlying layers of clay and gravel soil. Top layers of soil slip off the lower layers, or the clay layers can slip off each other, causing slides.

In January, 1969, heavy rain fell in coastal areas of California for nine days in a row. During that time, 10 inches (25 cm) of rain fell. Mudslides began to fall in the hills of San Gabriel and Santa Monica, near Los Angeles. Rivers of mud ran down the hills and washed away houses and cars.

At the same time, Santiago Creek filled with water from the rainstorms and mud from the mudslides. People who lived nearby

A landslide has made these houses in California slide down the hill.

tried to build a wall to keep the river from flooding their town, but this did not work. Finally, the United States Marines used helicopters to pick up cars that were smashed by the mudslides. They built a wall by stacking the cars along the river. This wall of cars stopped the flood from reaching the town.

Scientists study past slides like this one to predict where future landslides may form.

STUDYING SLIDES

Many geologists study landslides and avalanches. A **geologist** is a scientist who studies the layers of our planet's rock and soil. They study the causes of the slides and try to find ways to figure out when and where slides might happen. They also study what kinds of weather might start slides in an area.

Scientists learn a great deal by studying landslides and avalanches from the past. They look at things that happened before the slides to figure out what may have caused them. They also keep track of changes people make to slopes of mountains and hills. All of this information helps them better understand slides.

▲ This scientist is studying the layers of a
snowpack to see if they are unstable.

Scientific Tools

Most information about slides comes from
geologists' field work. They travel to places
where slides happen. They take soil samples
and study the kind of earth or snow. They
also use maps and computers to make models
of places where landslides could happen.

They measure the amount of rain or snow that falls and enter it into the computer. The computer then shows them what kind of slide may form and where it would flow. Scientists use the computer to figure out what is likely to happen if changes are made to a slope.

Scientists study the temperature of snow layers on a hill or mountain to predict avalanches. To predict is to make an educated guess about when something will likely happen. Scientists put special thermometers in places where avalanches often happen. The thermometers connect to computers. Scientists use their computers to watch for temperatures that could cause avalanches.

Scientists also dig deep holes in the snow. They study the different layers of snow to see how well they are sticking together. They look to see if slipping snow layers are making the snowpack unstable. Sometimes scientists cause little avalanches to see how well the layers stick together.

Preventing Avalanches and Landslides

Scientists cannot stop every slide from happening, but they do have some ways to control them. People can look at maps to see where slides happen. They can use wire and cement to build big walls or fences in places where landslides and avalanches often happen. These walls hold some of the slide and keep it from falling farther down. Stopping some of the slide also helps slow it down.

People also try to guide landslides away from towns. They dig large pits in the path of slides. The pits stop some of the slide and slow down the fall.

Scientists stop deadly avalanches by starting small ones when there is no one there. Today, people fire small explosives into places where they think avalanches will happen. This triggers, or starts, an avalanche. Once the avalanche has stopped, the area is safe for people to hike or ski on once again.

Today, scientists know more about landslides and avalanches than ever before.

People built this wire fence to help hold dirt in place and prevent a landslide.

Scientists can tell how likely it is that slides will form in certain areas. They can warn people who live in these places. In 1985, the U.S. Geological Survey and the National Weather Service started the Debris-Flow Warning System for the San Francisco Bay area. Scientists keep close track of slopes and weather conditions there. They warn people in this area if it is likely that landslides will form. This may help save people's lives.

GLOSSARY

creep (KREEP)—a slow-moving landslide

expand (x-PAND)—to widen

geologist (gee-AHL-uh-gist)—a scientist who studies rocks, soils, and earth forms

gnome (NOME)—a small mythical creature believed to live in mountains

gravity (GRA-vi-tee)—a force that pulls objects toward the center of our planet

hypothermia (hye-poh-THERM-ee-uh)—a lower-than-normal body temperature

landslide (LAND-slide)—a mass of earth that slides downhill

mudslide (MUD-slide)—a landslide made mostly of mud

scar (SKAR)—a permanent mark from damage or an injury

slope (SLOHP)—to be at an angle

slump (SLUHMP)—a slow-moving piece of hillside that falls a short distance

steep (STEEP)—having a sharp rise or slope

unstable (uhn-STAY-buhl)—not fixed or firm

Avalanche Dogs
http://www.drizzle.com/~danc/avalanche.html

Colorado Avalanche Information Center
http://www.caic.state.co.us/facts.html

FEMA for Kids
http://www.fema.gov/kids

U.S. Geological Survey
http://www.usgs.gov

Colorado Avalanche Information Center
325 Broadway Street, WS#1
Boulder, CO 80303-3337

National Landslide Information Center
U.S. Geological Survey
Federal Center
P.O. Box 25046 MS 966
Denver, CO 80225

Index

ML   10/02